Federal
Coal Leasing
Policy

Federal Coal Leasing Policy

Competition in the Energy Industries

Richard L. Gordon

American Enterprise Institute for Public Policy Research
Washington and London

Richard L. Gordon is professor of mineral economics at the College of Earth and Mineral Sciences, The Pennsylvania State University.

ISBN 0–8447–3427–6

Library of Congress Catalog Number 81–67556

AEI Studies 326

Printed in the United States of America

Contents

Preface

Federal, state, and local regulations on the production, distribution, and use of energy resources increased so much during the 1970s that only a few specialists in the field can assess their full scope. Although the regulations that affect the production, distribution, and use of coal match the severity of regulations affecting other fuels, the stringency of coal regulations has attracted inadequate attention. This paper focuses on a particularly little known aspect of federal policy on coal production, namely, federal policy on the leasing of federally owned land containing coal deposits.

The views expressed in this paper are based both on a review of the literature cited in the bibliography and on the author's activities over several years pertaining to the economics of coal production, distribution, and use. These activities have included appraisals of coal supply models for the Electric Power Research Institute (EPRI), assistance of the Management Analysis Center, Inc., in the preparation of a report for a client that was objecting to the proposed Department of Justice guidelines, and participation in a symposium sponsored by the Department of the Interior on a definition of the fair market value of federally owned coal. In addition, the author visited coal producers around the country in the spring of 1980 to develop better models of the coal-supply process for EPRI. This manuscript was completed in the fall of 1980 and does not consider 1981 developments.

The assistance of Exxon U.S.A. in furthering this research and the aid of John Boatwright, its coordinator of economics, in particular, are gratefully acknowledged. The views expressed here, however, are the author's, and they do not necessarily correspond with those of other analysts of federal energy policy and regulations, including the organizations for whom I consulted. My secretary, Mrs. T. Fleming, as usual did an excellent job with the typing. The Center for Energy Policy Research at the Massachusetts Institute of Technology, where I am spending the 1980–1981 academic year, was extremely helpful in assisting the completion of the editorial work.

1

Introduction

The federal government owns a substantial portion of this country's coal resources, especially those west of the Mississippi River. The exact amount of total or federally owned resources is not known, however. The 1979 *Final Environmental Statement, Federal Coal Management Program* issued by the Department of the Interior's Bureau of Land Management indicates that federal coal resources are concentrated in Colorado, Montana, New Mexico, North Dakota, Utah, and Wyoming.[1] It is estimated that federal holdings constitute 72 percent of the coal reserves in these states. Since these states account for about 47 percent of the country's demonstrated coal reserves and about 88 percent of the western reserves, the respective federal shares are 34 percent and 62 percent.[2]

Federal ownership of coal, however, is complicated by several special circumstances. In the past the federal government made outright grants to western railroads of land adjacent to the land used for railroad rights of way, and much of this land is still in private hands. Moreover, these grants to railroads had the peculiarity of ceding only part of the land near rights of way to the railroads while the federal government retained the rest. Furthermore, the federal government has in many cases sold the surface rights to land in the West while retaining the mineral rights. In addition, a portion of the coal-bearing lands of the West is held by other private parties, by Indian tribes, or by state governments. This intermingling of land-ownership makes the exploitation of western coal reserves more difficult, since a parcel of land must be of an adequate size ("a logical

---

[1] U.S. Bureau of Land Management, *Final Environmental Statement, Federal Coal Management Program*, 1979, p. 2–1.

[2] Ibid., pp. 2–4, 2–5.

mining unit") if mining is to be carried out efficiently. Hence, parcels of land—or mining rights—must be secured from different owners to provide a land tract of optimum size. This means, in turn, that much of the nation's coal, particularly in the West, cannot be exploited unless private producers are granted access to the coal in federal ownership.[3]

In managing its substantial coal resources, the federal government has emphasized limiting economic rents (that is, the profits resulting from appreciation in the value of mineral properties) and preventing environmental damage. Indeed, the federal government has virtually stopped its leasing of land for coal production while developing stricter rules for mining on its lands, should leasing resume.

The present study contends that current federal policy should be changed and that it is preferable to lease as much federal land as possible for the production of coal. The primary basis of this argument is that fears of excessive economic rents are unjustified. Such fears reflect governmental concern about the development of energy monopoly. Extensive governmental and private analysis of allegations of a developing energy monopoly actually have greatly weakened the contention that anticompetitive behavior is widespread. The studies have indeed concluded that competition is vigorous.

A secondary governmental concern about private markets is that speculators will be excessively rewarded unless the government intervenes. It is argued here, however, that undue weight is being attached to this view and that too little attention is being paid to the socially valuable service provided by speculators.

Moreover, the government has been inadequately aware of its substantial abilities to eliminate economic rents. Through competitive leasing of coal lands, taxation imposed after coal mines have been developed, or a combination of the two, the federal government has the ability to capture the rents.

The government's preoccupation with limiting profits initially was expressed by a moratorium on the granting of new leases, which has been in effect since 1971. In addition, Congress passed the Coal Leasing Amendments Act of 1976 in part, ostensibly, for the purpose of promoting competition. The act involves such matters as how much coal land a company may lease and the speed at which the leases must be developed and requires assurance that the federal government will receive a "fair market value" (presumably meaning all of the economic rent) for its leases. Other provisions of the act are designed

---

[3] Scott L. Parker et al., *An Analysis of Aspects of the Department of Justice's May 1978 Report on "Competition in the Coal Industry"* (Washington, D.C.: Management Analysis Center, 1979), pp. 36–37.

2

to ensure efficient recovery of coal, to protect the rights of people who own the surface rights of coal-bearing lands, and to require that the Department of Justice actively promote competition in the coal industry.

It is argued here that most of these legislative provisions are unwise in principle and have been inappropriately applied in practice. Special emphasis is placed on the Justice Department's interpretation of its proper role. It is suggested that the true monopoly problem is that, probably inadvertently, the cumulative effect of government policy has been the development of a de facto governmental monopoly over coal (and oil and gas). Thus, the critical reform at this point is to reduce government monopoly by the resumption of extensive leasing and the removal of some of the legislative restrictions, or at least a more sensible interpretation of these laws by executive agencies.

The Justice Department has taken a dubious approach in appraising the competitive impact of leasing. The department's proposed guidelines on leasing constitute the conclusion to a report that evaluates competition in the coal industry. This analysis suggests that even if one defines the geographic scope of coal markets as narrowly as is reasonable, no evidence exists that severe anticompetitive pressures prevail. Nonetheless, the department then presents rigid guidelines designed to limit market shares. Moreover, the shares are related to the narrow markets as they were defined to permit a conservative estimate of the extent of competition. In short, an analytic device that would actually strengthen the case against federal intervention is employed to support guidelines that implicitly assume that strict controls are needed.

Appropriate guidelines are difficult to devise under any circumstances. The relevant market is usually hard to define, and no theoretic or empirical basis exists for defining critical shares. Furthermore, the Justice Department's guidelines introduced special problems. The department's chief concern was the share of total reserves that could be, but had not yet been, committed to buyers. Formidable measurement problems exist in determining both the amount of reserves that would be available to any firm and the total amount that would be available in each market. Coal holdings may be quite different from marketable reserves, and the degree of commitment to developing these reserves may be difficult to ascertain.

The preferable approach to ensuring competition would be to alter leasing policy to make considerably more coal available for development. If the government insists on constraining competition by limiting the leasing of coal lands, it may become necessary for the Justice Department to act to prevent those who hold the leases from

3

attaining a monopoly position. In terms of economic principles as well as common sense, no reason exists to assume that guidance should consist of mechanistic formulas of the kind proposed by the department. The logical implication of the analysis, reviewed below, by the Justice Department, the Federal Trade Commission, and the General Accounting Office is that only limited attention to preventing private monopoly is necessary. The guidelines, however, hardly meet that description. If explicit guidelines need to be formulated, the Justice Department ought to consider less stringent ones. The analysis undertaken here, however, suggests that it is unlikely that sensible rules can be devised.

It is also argued here that the environmental policies that have been applied to the mining of coal on federal lands tend to be more cumbersome than necessary to attain given goals. The validity of some of the goals themselves is also questioned.

2
Coal Leasing: Goals and the Participants in Policy Making

Economists recognize that private markets have defects, such as an inherent inability to solve environmental problems, that sometimes justify government intervention in those markets. Many observers of our current environmental policies, however, now suggest that financial incentives—such as the imposition of emission-based taxes on polluters—may be preferable to the regulation that has been adopted by the federal government.

Economists also recognize a widespread tendency to disparage the market for being too effective and thus damaging a particular interest group—particularly one business interest harmed by another. Thus, government regulation must strike a balance between control over imperfections and the prevention of unneeded intervention.

For many years the latter concern dominated energy economics. Before 1970 economists saw the key problem as undue governmental concern for small firms in the extraction of oil, natural gas, and coal and in the refining of petroleum. Since then, however, the government's emphasis has been on restraining the activities of the large oil companies.

Energy economists tend to oppose most existing restrictions on the energy industries except for environmental controls and federal efforts to offset the impact of any disruption in the supply of imported oil. A wide range of views prevails on these two issues. Some leading energy economists are quite supportive of environmental controls, while others believe that existing regulatory policies need considerable reform.[1]

---

[1] Robert Stobaugh and Daniel Yergin, eds., *Energy Future* (New York: Random House, 1979), present a discussion generally sympathetic to environmental controls. Hans H. Landsberg et al., *Energy: The Next Twenty Years* (Cambridge, Mass.: Ballinger, 1979), is severely critical of existing environmental policies.

The basic objection to many environmental policies is that the government attempts to impose much too specific control on an industry. The regulators assume that they have a much better knowledge of the inner workings of an industry than they possess or are ever likely to attain. Thus, instituting appropriate financial pressures to attain environmental goals would allow private firms, with their superior knowledge of the costs of alternative compliance strategies, to find the cheapest ways to reduce environmental damage. The regulator's problem then becomes one of determining whether the financial pressure is sufficient. By making the potential savings high enough for firms that comply, the regulator can then ensure the attainment of environmental goals.

Economists stress the point that profit-seeking behavior can produce important social benefits. Economists also emphasize that it is possible to overdo anything, including the pursuit of health, safety, or environmental protection. If too much is spent in pursuing these goals, too little may be left for other goals, such as alleviating poverty or reducing unemployment.

The Goals of Federal Energy Policy

The chief stated goals of federal energy policy long have been (1) to promote the efficient production of energy resources, (2) to prevent excessive profits from accruing to the producers, and (3) to protect the environment and public health and safety. The achievement of these goals became more problematic in the 1970s, however, because of an apparent search for certainty. Policy makers today often purport to demand from technical experts the assurance that laws and regulations pertaining to energy policy will infallibly achieve these three goals, and they claim to assume that such assurances can be provided through complex mathematical analyses performed by computers. It is an elementary principle of logic, however, that such analyses only trace the consequences of the assumptions on which they are based. Every builder of the mathematical models used in these analyses is aware that his model contains many ill-verified assumptions. Hence, perfect forecasts of the effects of policy decisions are unattainable.

In some cases the request for assurance may be a way to prevent action, that is, by arguing that in view of the inherently inconclusive nature of forecasts, we do now know enough to take action. Conversely, if action is strongly desired, the defects of the model will be overlooked, and the results of the calculations using the model will be cited as conclusive evidence that a particular policy will prove beneficial. Thus, requests for assurance frequently appear to be more a part of political maneuvering than honest pleas for guidance.

The conflicts among energy production, profit restriction, and environmental protection are more familiar, and the implications are more obvious. Environmental regulations, for example, should discourage coal production whose costs, including those of environmental damage, exceed the market price that can be obtained for the coal.

In principle, no conflict need exist between profit limitation and efficient production. It is a standard proposition of the economics of taxation that a tax or charge levied on so-called excess profits (that is, those greater than needed to attract resources into an industry) or economic rents will have no effect on output.[2] The basic problem is that most of the actual methods of limiting profits fail to capture the rents and manage to discourage output.

The argument for taxes on economic rents is virtually a tautology. Those who offer goods or services for sale have a minimum price at which they will sell a given quantity of those goods or services. If the offerers receive at least that price, they will provide the given quantity. A rent, then, is the difference between what is paid and what the sellers would have settled for to provide the given quantity. A rent is unrequired payment and thus can be safely taxed.

Since we rarely can know the true required price, however, we cannot tell how much income is excess income. For example, the elaborate efforts of financial analysts to figure out the true cost of capital have proved to be quite imperfect. Accountants refuse to attempt to subdivide profit, as they define it, between required repayments to investors and rents earned. The deficiencies of the efforts of financial analysts to develop a satisfactory method of isolating the rent component of accounting profits suggest that policy makers do not have the tools to measure economic rents accurately and tax them only.

The problem is exacerbated by the tendency to use methods of taxation that are known to interfere with efficient production. Almost invariably, a charge on the percentage of gross income is imposed (for example, a sales tax, a royalty, or the tax on U.S. oil production levied on the difference between allowable and actual prices but misleadingly called an excess profits tax). Such taxes must be paid whether or not excess profits are really earned. They therefore dis-

---

[2] Richard A. Musgrave, *The Theory of Public Finance* (New York: McGraw-Hill, 1959), pp. 277–78.

courage production when the tax reduces income below the amount necessary to repay costs.

A nondistortionary method of taxation does in fact exist. Firms know what their true costs are and can make an offer to purchase mineral rights for a lump-sum payment that just allows recovery of all costs. Vigorous competition for mineral rights would guarantee that the offers would be raised to levels that would eliminate economic rents. Extensive studies of oil and gas leasing have consistently shown that this theoretically predicted result does occur in practice.[3]

Fears abound in some quarters that comparable competition does not exist in the coal industry and that the bids accepted for leases would be less successful in capturing economic rents. These fears seem inappropriate, however, since several government and private studies have concluded that the coal industry is highly competitive.[4] The entry of a wide variety of oil companies, electric utilities, established coal-mining companies, construction companies, and others into the market for western coal rights has made the competition vigorous. There would probably be even more competitors seeking entry were it not for the inability to operate profitably all the capacity now in existence. Despite the overall lack of growth in eastern coal mining, newcomers have arisen there, too.

Another key aspect of energy policy making in the 1970s, however, was to reduce reliance on the nondistortionary method of rent capture cited above—lump-sum payments for mining rights. Another major objective has been to limit the role of larger companies—particularly the major oil companies.[5]

The Role of Speculation

One concern frequently expressed about coal leasing is that too much leased land containing coal will be held for speculative purposes. Speculators consist of all those who hold resources for future use. Some speculators expect to produce the resources themselves, while others intend to resell the rights when conditions are appropriate. In

---

[3] See Walter Mead et al., *Competition and Performance in OCS Oil and Gas Lease Sales and Lease Development, 1954–1969* (Reston, Va.: U.S. Geological Survey, 1980).

[4] The government studies are discussed below, in chapter 5. The principal private study is Thomas D. Duchesneau, *Competition in the U.S. Energy Industry* (Cambridge, Mass.: Ballinger, 1975).

[5] See Stephen L. McDonald, *The Leasing of Federal Lands for Fossil Fuels Production* (Baltimore: Johns Hopkins University Press for Resources for the Future, 1979), for a review of leasing policy that includes extensive review of the trend toward use of more distortionary methods of charging.

many discussions of coal leasing, oddly enough, producer holdings have been more vigorously attacked. Given the alleged desire to encourage production, critics of speculation might logically consider even less desirable those speculators who plan to resell their holdings.

The role of speculators who hold coal-bearing land for resale actually is to provide a special expertise that is not efficiently provided by firms that specialize in production. Land speculators amass an intimate knowledge of the availability of land in a particular area and thus a superior ability to assess how best to assemble parcels of land that can be mined or otherwise efficiently employed. Given the scattered landholding noted at the start of this study, speculators may be essential to the efficient aggregation of coal properties into parcels that can be efficiently mined. Speculators also provide additional competition for leases.

Speculation generally contributes to more efficient production. The role of speculation is to overcome the problems that limit the development of production. The speculator has cleared many of the administrative barriers well in advance of production and makes it easier to respond to demands as they arise, since what is needed is land parcels on which mines can be quickly developed. Clearly, then, the greater the administrative barriers to resource acquisition and development, the more speculation is desirable.

But federal coal policy, in its insistence upon increasing the administrative barriers to securing and putting a lease into operation, also makes it more difficult to hold leases. These actions combine to reduce the ability of producers to produce coal. No sensible justification exists for such restrictions. Given the limits (which are outlined below) on the holdings of any one firm, the addition of limits on total industry holdings is unnecessary and may even be anticompetitive. Limits on the holdings of individual firms should suffice to create numerous firms, none of which can control prices.

As far as economic efficiency is concerned, leasing can be inadequate but never deficient. If a company leases land where the exploitation of coal resources is not presently competitive, no harm results because the land will simply not be mined (unless the government adds, as it has, pressure to mine the land prematurely). But a failure to lease coal resources whose mining would have been profitable irreversibly raises costs.

The problem of environmental protection does not by itself affect this conclusion. If good environmental policies exist, the decision of leaseholders on whether to begin exploitation will involve a consideration of environmental costs, and production that should be prevented for environmental reasons will be prevented. Similarly, the level of leasing, for reasons discussed below, should not greatly affect the transfer of economic rents to the government.

The effect of governmental limits on leasing is exacerbated by the forecasting burden it places on government. It becomes necessary for the government to determine which reserves will be needed and when. It is doubtful that the federal government both could and would assemble the data that would be needed for such predictions. Limited leasing is likely to be particularly inappropriate for the 1980s, since conditions in the energy market are likely to remain highly unsettled and subject to continued disturbances (including further governmental changes in the ground rules). Thus, limiting leasing to what the government determines to be "requirements" is infeasible as well as undesirable. The process assigns more decision-making authority to public policy makers than they can manage.

The market appears to be better at determining the optimum pattern of development of coal supply than any conceivable governmental decision-making process. Experience shows that Congress is rarely willing to appropriate the funds necessary for the types of extensive analysis that would be required to determine the best constraints on leasing.

Given that the federal government is so substantial a landowner, it possesses substantial monopoly power that should be restrained. Federal limitations on leasing can prove to abet use of that monopoly power. The government's authority to limit leasing can be used to justify the sale of less coal than would be desirable from the viewpoint of economic efficiency. In particular, the government can keep off the market coal resources that should be developed because their cost, including environmental damage, is less than the price at which they can be sold. This restriction on supply will then raise the price of coal and, in turn, what bidders will be willing to pay for leases. In this way the government can both create and capture substantial monopoly profits. The effort to prevent excess gains by private individuals or firms threatens to lead to much larger excess gains by the only well-identified possessor of true monopoly power in coal, namely, the federal government.

If the goal is to ensure the vigor of competition, there can never be too many owners of mineral rights. Overzealous efforts to curtail the total amount of leasing may not only reduce the availability of coal but also give part of the government's monopoly power to a restricted group of leaseholders. Competitive bidding will ensure that adequate payments will be made, and this process should not be materially affected by the possibility that not all of the leases will be exploited immediately. A well-functioning market will ensure that the bids are properly adjusted to take account of this uncertainty.

The concept of a well-functioning market includes the belief that a profitable investment can always be financed. Those familiar with the literature on investment behavior know that some theorists allege that methods of pooling risks among a variety of institutions are inadequate to command enough investment in highly risky alternatives. But financial institutions have shown considerable ingenuity in devising new techniques to meet new needs. What seems to bother some theorists is that, contrary to their theories, actual institutions do not provide all the necessary risk-pooling devices. The real defect seems to lie in the theories, which assume that the creation of such devices is costless. Financial institutions cost money to operate, and the financial community stops short of providing complete risk pooling because the additional cost would be more than the likely benefit. Thus, this theoretical criticism of capital markets seems misplaced.

It is true, of course, that the government would receive less gross income under rapid leasing than it would if it delayed leasing. This would not be a loss, however, but merely a reflection of the fact that money earns interest. The purchase of a lease before exploitation means that the purchaser surrenders money and therefore forgoes interest on it. Conversely, the government gains the opportunity to earn interest during the period between the sale and exploitation. The lower price for an earlier purchase should exactly equal the interest forgone by the government. The government's ability to earn interest means that, if it reinvested the income for the sale of a lease whenever leasing occurred, it would end up with exactly the same gross income at the time mining starts.[6] At that time, the initial payment plus accrued interest would be identical and equal to the present value of the economic rents.

Another way to ensure the capture of economic rents would be to impose additional taxes once the total rents were known. To be sure, these taxes would distort production to a greater extent than lump-sum payments would. In the 1970s, however, Congress showed little concern about imposing highly distortionary taxes.

In sum, so-called excess leaseholding proves, on close examination, to be a virtue. No marked social harm can result from leasing coal lands well before their actual development. Furthermore, the failure to lease the best land means that inferior coal land will be mined. Public policies designed to restrict either the total amount of land

---

[6] Ibid., p. 89, presents a contrary view on the issue of limited leasing and a citation of a communication from Walter Mead supporting my position.

under lease or the period for which the land may be leased are therefore ill advised. Moreover, government lacks the ability to develop the accurate forecasts needed to make limited leasing work satisfactorily.

Any special action directed at speculative holdings of land by middlemen is equally ill advised. The widespread prejudice against such speculators is due in large measure to complaints by other businesses that speculation destabilizes markets, which probably means in the case of federal land leasing and most other situations that speculation makes markets more competitive.

Protecting the Rights of Surface Owners

Protection of the owners of surface rights to mineral lands is a justifiable public concern. Appropriate protective devices are quite difficult to devise, however, particularly in the context of restrictive leasing policies. A badly designed program would allow the owners of surface rights to preempt governmental collection of economic rents. As noted, competitive, well-informed bidders for mineral rights are willing to pay an amount up to the present value of the economic rents for access to mineral rights. If the law allows surface owners to sell before the government, the surface owners can capture the rents. This, of course, would undermine the principle that the government should receive the rents. Reliance on postlease negotiations with surface owners could prevent this but still could, under inappropriate institutional arrangement, give the surface owners a degree of monopoly power.

Dangers like these are also aggravated by a policy of limited leasing. If leasing is extensive, each landowner is simply one of many possible suppliers of land, and competitive market forces will lead to the appropriate sale price, namely, the value of the land for whatever its most profitable alternative use may be. In recognition of the problem of rent capture by surface landowners, the Interior Department has proposed to limit what owners of surface rights may charge for those rights.

This review indicates that the desire to limit the total number and duration of leases of federal coal lands to private interests is likely to harm competition, may impede the expeditious development of energy resources, and will not contribute much, if anything, to capturing economic rents.[7]

---

[7] Whether existing requirements for the reclamation of surface mines benefit or harm the public interest remains controversial and is, in any event, not central to the concerns expressed here.

The Participants in the Debates on Leasing Policy

Federal policies affecting coal production and use have emerged from an elaborate but largely uncoordinated process of interaction among government agencies, Congress, lobbyists for energy interests, environmental groups, and organized critics of the energy industries.[8] Three basic points should be made about this process. First, the resulting institutional framework is quite complex, probably unnecessarily so.[9] Second, none of the interested groups is monolithic. Third, no warrant exists for considering any of these groups more selfless than the others.

The rifts within the various interested groups are considerable, but they are probably most obvious in the case of the producers. Some of the independent coal companies complain privately about the entry of oil companies and other types of business firms into the industry, while eastern coal interests seek to restrain competition from western coal interests. At least some electric utilities (most notably the Tennessee Valley Authority) have joined the attack on energy monopolies.[10]

The critical concern here, however, is not that these different groups exist and have had various degrees of success in influencing policy making. What is more important here is an understanding of the wide variety of federal agencies that directly or indirectly affect coal leasing. Attention must be given both to the agencies that control coal supply and to those that affect the level and composition of coal demand. In ways that are difficult to predict, the agencies that affect demand thus alter the amount of federal coal that can be exploited.

As coal-leasing policy evolved in the 1970s, a wide variety of federal participants became involved, making use of both long-established legislation and new laws. The Department of the Interior remains the focal point for most of the critical decisions, but authority within the department has become increasingly dispersed. The department's Bureau of Land Management and the U.S. Geological Survey continue to hold their longstanding responsibilities to implement

[8] The term "organized critics" refers to so-called consumer groups. I believe these groups are poor representatives of consumers, but no neutral term to identify them is in general circulation.

[9] See Landsberg, *Energy*, passim, esp. chap. 14; and Daniel M. Ogden, Jr., "Protecting Energy Turf: The Department of Energy Organization Act," *Natural Resources Journal*, vol. 18 (October 1978), pp. 845–57.

[10] See U.S. Tennessee Valley Authority, *The Structure of the Energy Markets: A Report of TVA's Antitrust Investigation of the Coal and Uranium Industries* (Knoxville, 1977), and *The Structure of the Energy Markets: A Report of TVA's Antitrust Investigation of the Coal and Uranium Industries, 1979 Update* (Knoxville, 1979).

policy. Leasing is primarily a function of the Bureau of Land Management, while the Geological Survey has the major authority to appraise resources. The Office of Surface Mining, created in 1977, has responsibility for regulating strip mining, including the mining of coal that is federally owned. Meanwhile, the Bureau of Indian Affairs has become more assertive in helping Indian tribes to obtain better contracts for coal on tribal lands and to renegotiate earlier contracts now alleged to be unsatisfactory. The proliferation of Interior Department obligations, moreover, has led to the creation of several ad hoc task forces.

Furthermore, the secretary of the interior and his assistants were compelled to devote considerable attention during the 1970s to leasing questions.[11]

Other government agencies that have become directly involved in leasing policy include the Department of Energy, which is charged with setting the basic goals of the leasing program, and the Department of Justice, which has proposed guidelines to ensure that current leasing procedures avoid anticompetitive effects. Important indirect influences include the Environmental Protection Agency, which establishes rules governing the burning of coal, and the Interstate Commerce Commission and the Department of Transportation, whose regulations affect the costs of transporting coal.

Congress has been involved in leasing policy by enacting the legislation that created new responsibilities for the agencies mentioned. The implementation of many of these laws has been challenged in the federal courts by such groups as the Sierra Club and the National Resources Defense Council, and as a result the courts have also become a factor in leasing policy.

---

[11] The longstanding DOI responsibility to regulate coal-mining operations to protect the health and the safety of miners was transferred to the Department of Labor in 1978.

3

An Examination of Major Decisions Affecting Coal Leasing

In 1971 Interior Secretary Rogers C. B. Morton imposed a moratorium on the leasing of federal land for the mining of coal. Subsequent efforts of the Department of the Interior to lift the moratorium have been hampered by various laws enacted by Congress, most of them for the purpose of protecting the environment.

The moratorium limited the issuance of leases to those necessary to the continued operation of existing mines. As of early 1981 a resumption of full-scale leasing was scheduled for later in 1981. The Reagan administration appears eager to speed leasing.

The moratorium has been rationalized somewhat differently in various reviews of the matter. For example, the Department of the Interior's *Final Environmental Statement, Federal Coal Management Program* traces the moratorium to a 1970 report by the Bureau of Land Management surveying the history of leasing.[1] The survey showed a sharp increase (from 80,000 to 788,000 acres) in the amount of land under lease in 1970 as compared with 1945, but it also showed a decline in coal production on these lands. The Department of Interior therefore concluded that further leasing could be safely delayed, and a similar argument was made in a 1974 report by a private group called the Council on Economic Priorities. In 1978 the Department of Justice issued a report on competition in the coal industry that cited the Interior Department's reason for the moratorium but placed more emphasis on assertions also made in the report by the Council on Economic Priorities that too little had been charged for the leases.[2]

These views now seem curious. Leasing occurs for the purpose of

---

[1] See U.S. Bureau of Land Management, *Final Environmental Statement, Federal Coal Management Program*, 1979, pp. 1–9.

[2] See U.S. Department of Justice, *Competition in the Coal Industry*, 1978, p. 3.

satisfying anticipated future demands for coal, and what was important was the prospect of an expansion of demand. The possibility that demand would, in fact, increase was clearly observable at the time the moratorium was imposed. Commonwealth Edison and other midwestern utilities had started using low-sulfur western coal, and concern was rising among the utilities that stack-gas scrubbers to remove sulfur dioxide from the air emissions of plants using high-sulfur coal would cost more than increased use of western coal. The signs of a growing demand for western coal, of course, have become more widely evident since then.

The laws that have significantly influenced federal leasing policy include the National Environmental Policy Act (NEPA) of 1969, the Coal Leasing Amendments Act of 1976, the Surface Mining Control and Reclamation Act of 1977, the Clean Air Act Amendments of 1977, and the Department of Energy Act of 1977.

The key element of the NEPA was the requirement that all major federal actions be accompanied by environmental impact statements to show that the programs would be conducted in compliance with federal environmental goals. In practice, however, requiring environmental impact statements has been an effective way of preventing rapid action and an ineffective way of promoting environmental improvement.

The basic problem is that the NEPA substitutes formalistic review by unqualified observers for substantive control by appropriate authorities. The courts have developed an elaborate set of guidelines about what constitutes an adequate environmental impact statement, but there is little evidence that these guidelines ensure proper action. Indeed, the guidelines seem to have headed the impact statement process and the application of environmental rules to governmental actions in the worst possible direction.

As interpreted by the courts, the NEPA requires each agency to determine which alternative decision in any particular case would be environmentally preferable. Under these guidelines, every agency must pretend to have the competence to appraise a wide variety of alternatives. Every decision relating to a specific type of energy, for example, must include a determination of whether some other source of energy would be a better choice.

The minimum complaint about this process is that it is almost certain to be ill performed. It is quite unlikely that funds will be appropriated to permit the acquisition of sufficient expertise to permit an adequate appraisal.

More fundamental problems exist, however. In terms of efficient and consistent administration, it is undesirable to make each agency an independent judge of what is environmentally appropriate. Federal agencies ought to be subject to the same sorts of pressure that ideally would be applied to private parties. Federal regulatory bodies would set up well-defined environmental goals and develop effective methods of ensuring compliance. The rule-making agencies, in their turn, ought to have well-defined congressional mandates to guide their decisions. Such mandates would make environmental impact statements unnecessary.

It now appears that with sufficient diligence any aggrieved party can find a judge willing to find flaws in any given environmental impact statement. Some statements go unchallenged while others are successfully blocked. Thus, in 1977 a federal court held that the Interior Department's environmental impact statement on the proposed resumption of coal leasing failed to consider adequately the alternative of no leasing. The court decision appeared illogical, since the department's statement only sought permission to consider what might constitute the optimal level of leasing. Since nonleasing is simply setting the optimum level at zero, the search for an optimum implicitly involved a consideration of nonleasing. The decision might have been overturned through an appeal to a higher court, but the department chose not to make such an appeal. Cases like this suggest, therefore, that the NEPA should be replaced by the approach outlined above.

Another important influence on leasing policy is the Coal Leasing Amendments Act of 1976. The amendments combined federal offers of additional funds to coal-mining states with the imposition of a variety of restrictions on the terms of leaseholdings. One of these restrictions was that a 12.5 percent royalty had to be one element of the payments leaseholders made to the federal government. The fresh grant to the states then was half that royalty income. Presumably this provision was added to make the bill more appealing to mining state members of Congress. (Another 40 percent of royalty income has traditionally been earmarked for federal projects in the states where federal lands are leased and mined.)

The restrictions include rules on the terms of leasing and the amounts of land that individuals can hold, upper limits on the period between the granting of a lease and the start of coal production, and rules on mine operation. The leasing policy restrictions include the suggestion that efforts should be made by the Bureau of Land Management to ensure that any given tract of land is large enough to support an economically efficient mine (but does not exceed 25,000 acres). At least half of the leases must be granted under a system in which the buyer can defer paying the lump sum ordinarily required as part of the compensation to the government. The amendments also include a provision that requires the setting-aside of some leases for small businesses and public bodies. Under the newly amended law, the government was expected to receive fair market value for all of the coal found on the leased land. Fair market value was undefined in the act but apparently was to be interpreted as meaning the full capture of economic rents.

The legislation limits a firm to 40,000 acres per state and 100,000 acres nationally and precludes leasing to firms that have not started producing coal from land previously leased. Exploitation must begin within ten years of the granting of the lease, and reserves may not exceed the amount that could be produced within forty years. Other provisions of the act, discussed below, required the Interior Department to estimate the most desirable production rate for the property. The department subsequently indicated that holders of coal rights previously leased but not put into production by June 1, 1986, could lose their leases. Firms were required to maximize the recovery of coal, and the Department of Justice was given the task of monitoring the effect of leasing policy on competition among coal producers through both an annual report on the status of competition and assessments of whether given leases "would create or maintain a situation inconsistent with the antitrust laws." (The monitoring of competition is discussed at greater length in chapter 4.)

Other provisions effectively shifted the responsibility for exploration to the federal government. Although exploration permits could be secured by private parties, there was no assurance that land that proved to contain coal deposits could be leased. Meanwhile, a resource appraisal program was to be instituted by the Geological Survey.

Due Diligence, Fair Market Value, and Maximum Economic Recovery

Further comments on due diligence (that is, the requirements for rapid development and limited lives for leases) and examination of the concepts of fair market value, maximum economic recovery, and similar requirements of the act are in order at this point.

It was argued above that no threat is posed either to economic efficiency or to the capture of excess profits by allowing leased land to stand unutilized. Conversely, however, restrictions on how long the leased land may be left idle and on the length of the production period can interfere with efficient use.

Due diligence, fair market value, and maximum economic recovery share the basic characteristic that they are innocuous only

18

when they are irrelevant to private decision making. No harm would be done by requirements of due diligence if optimum exploitation complied with the rules or if a particular lease was not worth exploiting. But if the most efficient extraction schedule came into conflict with the requirements of due diligence, harm would occur. Two outcomes are possible when the production timetable dictated by due diligence is inefficient. If the inefficiency is great enough, it will not be profitable to operate a mine, and the coal will not be available at the appropriate time unless the Interior Department has the extraordinary luck to issue a lease again when optimum development complies with the due diligence requirements. If the inefficiency is of a lesser degree, the leased land will be mined but with a suboptimal pattern of development. In particular, both excess production and profit reduction will probably occur.[3] Early in 1980 I interviewed the executives of numerous coal producers and found that those with leases in the West were developing them somewhat sooner than they desired simply to preserve the leases.

Fair market value and maximum economic recovery are principles that are satisfied automatically in a competitive market. The case for fair market value was made in the earlier discussion of how economic rents can be captured by competitive leasing. The point about full recovery is even simpler to make: a profit-seeking firm will naturally be motivated to recover all of the coal that can be recovered efficiently.

The best approach would be to assume that both goals will be automatically satisfied by market forces and not adopt specific enforcement procedures. Unfortunately, however, a law creates a presumption that action is needed, and the Interior Department has acted. In the case of maximum economic recovery, the response thus far has been appropriate. The department backed away from forcing producers to use some of their excess profits to subsidize the recovery of more expensive coal and is effectively allowing private firms to extract only the coal that is profitable to produce.[4] There is still the danger, however, that it will try to second-guess private estimates of profitability.

The department has spent some effort on trying to outguess the market in estimating fair market values, however, by developing a computer model with which it hopes to calculate such values and thus reject bids that fail to meet its estimates. For reasons discussed earlier,

---

[3] See Stephen L. McDonald, *The Leasing of Federal Lands for Fossil Fuels Production* (Baltimore: Johns Hopkins University Press for Resources for the Future, 1979), p. 89.

[4] See U.S. Department of the Interior, *Secretarial Issue Document: Federal Coal Management Program*, p. 17.

however, there is little reason for the department to put its trust in models.

The deferral of the lump-sum payment in partial compensation for leases was designed to increase the ability of smaller firms to participate in coal production. Presumably such firms can more easily finance several smaller payments than one big one. One might fairly ask whether western mining, where one mine could make its owner one of the top ten or twenty producers nationally, is a business for people so poorly financed that they cannot pay the lump sum immediately. On the other hand, no obvious harm is likely to be produced by the provision, which may provide some incentive for useful experimentation.

The final element of these efforts to alter the allocation of resources to coal that requires review is the suggestion that the Interior Department attempt to consolidate holdings into logical mining units. The concern is whether such efforts would be unnecessary and possibly inefficient because of the superior skill of private speculators.

Other Laws Affecting Leasing

Other laws affecting western coal development have had more indirect effects on leasing policy. The Surface Mine Control and Reclamation Act is important for making surface mining more difficult in several respects. The most familiar, and thus one that can be treated briefly, is that of imposing reclamation requirements. For the purpose of evaluating leasing policy, it suffices to note that the regulations under the act impose restrictions on mining practices that raise costs and thus weaken the competitive position of surface-mined coal. Coal producers have strongly argued that too mechanistic an approach to reclamation—invariably described as a "cookbook" method—has been taken, while environmentalists have expressed some concern about the weakness of the reclamation requirements.

The more interesting provisions are the unsuitability criteria and the surface landowner protection clauses. The unsuitability criteria mandate the elimination of surface mining in critical areas, such as national forests, prime agricultural lands, and alluvial valleys (essentially locations in which water flows occur that are essential to farming). General questions can be raised about the wisdom of so sweeping a set of provisions, and complaints are being heard that the alluvial valley prohibition is being interpreted in such a way that the slightest disruption of water flow is deemed cause for prohibiting mining. The clauses that protect surface landowners provide such owners with double protection. They can argue for exclusion of their land from exploitation, and they are guaranteed adequate compensation for any land disruption they allow.

The 1977 amendments to the Clean Air Act require the use of the best available control technology and the prevention of significant deterioration in air quality. The latter was the legislative ratification of a judicially created policy. The preamble to the Clean Air Act set preservation of air quality as a goal. Subsequently a federal judge decided this provision meant that it was necessary to limit increases in pollution in areas where air quality was better than that required by federal standards. The Environmental Protection Agency (EPA) proved incapable of implementing so vague a guideline, and Congress therefore included in the 1977 amendments a basis for setting policy to limit increases in pollution.

Just what the effect of the legislation will be remains to be seen. The impression one often gleans from casual discussions is that the legislation was intended to protect areas celebrated for their clean air, such as Arizona and New Mexico. In fact, prevention of significant deterioration (PSD) areas exist throughout the United States. Several eastern utilities have noted in their regular reports to the Securities and Exchange Commission that PSD rules are affecting plant-siting. New power plants and coal mines will compete for a share of the limited increments in pollution allowable with PSD, and their ability to locate in any PSD region will be limited. Disputes may thus arise between the builders of power plants for local use and the operators of mines or power plants in one region that are intended to serve another region.

The rules mandating the use of the best available control technology (BACT) pose a greater threat to western coal development than the creation of PSD areas. Many observers have said that the BACT requirement was largely a political attempt to limit western coal output that has only limited relevance to controlling air pollution.[5] Before 1977 new large coal-burning facilities were subject to rules that required the reduction of sulfur dioxide emissions to 1.20 pounds per million British thermal units (B.t.u.) burned. This stimulated greater demand for low-sulfur western coal and less use of emission cleanup devices than eastern coal interests expected. The BACT requirement was intended to result in the removal of sulfur from coal by precombustion cleaning or the capture of sulfur dioxide

---

[5] See Hans H. Landsberg et al., *Energy: The Next Twenty Years* (Cambridge, Mass.: Ballinger, 1979), p. 378, for a statement on the political intentions of the BACT requirement by his highly circumspect study group.

emissions by stack-gas scrubbers. Scrubbers, in fact, were expected to be the principal means of compliance, as shown by the EPA's emphasis on scrubber use in its policy studies.

One obvious concern of the EPA's in implementing the 1977 amendments was to guarantee that the new rules would not be less stringent than the old ones. Some types of coal contain so much sulfur that burning them would result in emissions that would systematically exceed the limit of 1.20 pounds of sulfur oxides per million B.t.u., despite the installation of high-performance scrubbers. To keep pollution levels below those required by the old rules, the new rules had to prohibit the burning of high-sulfur coal.

Another EPA concern was whether or not it was appropriate totally to ignore the advantages of using low-sulfur coal. Here the alternatives ranged from granting maximum possible credit for using low-sulfur coal to granting no credit. Full credit would have meant interpreting the BACT requirement as a mandate to tighten the emission limits to, say, 0.80 pounds per million B.t.u. Almost all coal emissions would have to be scrubbed, but the degree of scrubbing would be proportional to the sulfur content. At the other extreme, the emission difference could be ignored in favor of removing an equal percentage of sulfur from all types of coal.

The compromise adopted was that maximum scrubbing could be avoided if emissions were kept below 0.60 pounds. This standard has apparently provided only modest incentives for the scrubbing of low-sulfur coal.[6]

The creation of the Department of Energy produced still another complication in the establishment of coal-leasing policy. The department was only granted authority to establish overall leasing policy, while the Interior Department retained responsibility for administering the actual leasing process. But the border between policy and implementation is ill defined, and there has been friction over the extent to which the Department of Energy can exert its influence over the Interior Department.

One last complication has been the substantial increase in freight rates for coal transported by rail. Some observers suspect that the railroads have adopted a policy by which shippers with few transportation alternatives are being charged monopoly rates, shippers with several alternatives are getting more favorable rates, and excessive

---

[6] See Richard L. Gordon, *Economic Analysis of Coal Supply: An Assessment of Existing Studies* (Palo Alto: Electric Power Research Institute, 1979), vol. 3, chap. 2. This work relies heavily on reports by ICF, Inc.

rates are being charged to coal shippers to finance unprofitable lines whose abandonment is politically infeasible.[7]

The Results of Recent Federal Decisions

The legislation and administrative procedures discussed above have produced the following results:

First, new coal leasing is unlikely to resume before 1981.

Second, the review and approval procedure is now so long that it is likely to take a private enterprise ten years or more to move from a decision to operate a mine on federal land to the opening of the mine.

Third, the limits on total amounts of land leased and the due diligence provisions are anticompetitive and encourage economic inefficiency, as do current tax policies and the policy on setting aside land for particular groups.

Thus, the federal government—particularly Congress and certain regulatory agencies—has strongly discouraged competition in the coal industry. A true desire for greater competition would lead to the conclusion (a view already reached by the Department of Justice and the General Accounting Office) that if the federal government wants more competition in the coal industry, it should simply lease more federal land containing coal deposits.

---

[7] See statement by George H. Borts in *Statements of Facts and Argument of Union Electric Company, Wisconsin Electric Company, Wisconsin Power & Light Company, and Wisconsin Public Service Corporation before the Interstate Commerce Commission, Increased Rates on Coal, Midwestern Railroad, August 1979* (docket 37246 and sub. nos. 1–6 and consolidated cases 37348 and 37353), pp. 4, 8–9.

4

Competition in the Coal Industry and the Department of Justice Guidelines

The guidelines on coal leasing proposed in 1978 by the Department of Justice (DOJ) are based both on the information available on the problem of energy monopoly and on general antitrust analysis and policy. Energy monopoly and antitrust policy are broad topics, and this section is limited to a discussion of the documents most germane to an appraisal of the guidelines. As far as energy monopoly is concerned, this means the DOJ study explaining its leasing guidelines and a Federal Trade Commission study that was a major source of data for the DOJ. A few other studies, including one by the General Accounting Office, are noted. The review of antitrust policy is limited to the principles explicitly stated by the DOJ in establishing its guidelines.

The Prevention of Monopoly

Concern over energy monopoly, of course, has existed ever since the attacks in the late nineteenth century on the Standard Oil trust. Intense consideration of possibly anticompetitive conditions in the energy market emerged again during the late 1960s because of growing instability in the energy markets. Numerous congressional hearings have dealt with alleged monopolies in each of the processes associated with a given fuel (such as extraction or refining), through vertical integration (such as participation in production, refining, and transportation of oil), or through horizontal integration (especially by ownership of more than one source of energy). As a result, various proposals have been made to prohibit vertical integration as well as the production of more than one fuel. Some efforts have also been made to restrict the degree of participation of any one company in any one activity, and it is prohibitions of this type in the realm of coal, and coal and nuclear energy combined, that are of concern here.

The development of the DOJ guidelines was an attempt to give explicit meaning to an unclear congressional mandate: preventing "a situation inconsistent with the antitrust law."[1] The DOJ has interpreted this to mean that it can apply standards to the coal industry that are stricter than those normally applied in enforcing the antitrust laws. This principle of greater stringency grew out of interpretations of similar powers granted to the DOJ to review the licensing of nuclear power plants. It was decided that a perception of danger could be used to justify action by the department even if no antitrust law was violated.

Just what criteria would be used to determine potential danger is not very clear, since both the decision by the Nuclear Regulatory Commission (NRC) cited as the basis for the principle of greater stringency and the restatement of the decision by the DOJ are cryptic. As the DOJ quoted the NRC, situations "which ran counter to the *policies* underlying the [antitrust laws], even where no actual violation of statute was made clear, would warrant remedial license conditions under [the law authorizing antitrust review of nuclear plants]" (the emphasis and the first bracketed term come from the DOJ report).[2] The DOJ's attempt to explain this runs as follows: "Thus, situations inconsistent with the antitrust laws or counter to the tenets underlying those laws may be prevented from reaching the point where society would suffer from their detrimental effects."[3] This would appear to be an assertion of unlimited power to stop actions in any area to which the inconsistency with antitrust principle applies if there is the slightest suspicion of an anticompetitive threat.

The potential for abuse of this power seems to have been realized in the principles used to develop the DOJ guidelines on the coal industry. Reiterating a familiar point in the antitrust literature, the department's 1978 report states that the prevention of new developments, such as mergers that lessen competition, are subject to stricter enforcement standards involving less conclusive demonstrations of damages than the standards applicable to controlling the monopoly power of existing firms. In 1969 the department attempted to tighten its limits on all types of mergers by devising guidelines on what constituted an allowable merger.

---

[1] The phrase apparently was introduced in the antitrust provisions, section 105 a(5) of the Atomic Energy Act, governing nuclear licenses and was incorporated into section 8 of the Coal Leasing Amendments Act of 1976.

[2] See U.S. Department of Justice, *Competition in the Coal Industry*, 1978, p. 3.

[3] Ibid., p. 6.

These 1969 rules take into account the degree of concentration within an industry (that is, the total share of market sales of the four largest firms), the market share of the acquiring firm, and the market share of the acquired firm. Two sets of guidelines were provided. The more stringent set was for industries where concentration was 75 percent or more. The other set was for industries with a lesser concentration. Both sets of guidelines caused the size of allowable acquisitions to decrease as the market share of the acquiring firm became larger. The starting point in highly concentrated industries was that a firm with 4 percent of the market could not acquire a firm with an equal or larger share of the market. If the acquiring firm had a market share of 15 percent or more, it could not buy firms with market shares of 1 percent or more. The scale for less concentrated industries limited acquisitions by firms with a 5 percent share to firms with less than 5 percent; a firm with a 15 percent share could acquire firms with less than a 3 percent share; only when a firm's share reached 25 percent would it be prevented from acquiring firms with shares of 1 percent or more.

Justice combined its 1969 guidelines with its concept of greater stringency in developing its proposed 1978 guidelines for coal leasing. The 1978 guidelines are based on three general principles:

1. No company will be allowed to lease more federal coal if it holds more than 15 percent of the "uncommitted nonfederal reserves" in the relevant market. "Nonfederal" here includes federal coal under lease; the relevant markets, as discussed below, are defined in the DOJ report.
2. A 10 percent limit will be applied to firms also engaged in uranium conversion or fuel-rod fabrication.
3. The existing prohibitions on coal leasing by railroads will be supplemented by a ban on leases to joint ventures that include railroads.

To be sure, the proposed guidelines are hedged by noting that what is being stated is a prima facie case that "creates a rebuttal presumption." Although this apparently means that exceptions to the rules will be made, the department's reply to a letter from the Exxon Corporation in which the company said it thought exceptions would be rare was simply a reiteration that the presumption would be rebuttable.[4]

Despite the Justice Department's action, neither economic theory nor empirical evidence provides a satisfactory basis for setting

---

[4] Exxon U.S.A. (W. T. Slick), 1979 letter to John H. Shenefield of the U.S. Department of Justice.

mechanical rules for the acquisition of new coal leases by existing firms. The idea that firms should not be allowed to attain too large a market share has often been advocated, but no consensus prevails about how to select the cutoff point actually adopted.[5] Markets are difficult to define unambiguously. The DOJ guidelines do not follow logically from either the department's legal mandate or its analysis of actual problems. After having argued that no serious monopoly problems existed, the department then set up guidelines that are designed to constrain lease grants severely.

The DOJ also erred by requiring the industry to disprove the assumptions underlying the guidelines. These assumptions are hardly so well justified that the burden of proof should rest on the companies; the Justice Department should be the one required to prove harm.

The guidelines are far less stringent, however, than some of the legislation that has been proposed to limit the participation of any one company to one stage in the production and processing of one fuel, as well as proposed bills that would simply ban oil companies from obtaining federal coal leases or uranium claims. An alternative, proposed by Alfred F. Dougherty of the Federal Trade Commission, would be to limit coal holdings by all oil companies to 5 percent of national reserves.[6]

Problems of Appraising Competition

For many years analysts of competition in the U.S. economy have employed "concentration ratios" as indicators of the vigor of competition within an industry. Periodically, efforts are made to establish rules of thumb about what constitutes a degree of concentration indicative of inadequate competition. Sometimes these measures are simply suggested as theoretical exercises, but occasionally proposals (such as those of the DOJ) are made to guide public policy according to such rules of thumb. Such proposals have received scant acclaim. No adequate basis exists for establishing such rules, which involve running roughshod over economic principles.

---

[5] See U.S. Federal Trade Commission, *Report to the Federal Trade Commission on the Structure of the Nation's Coal Industry*, 1978, pp. 32–35, for a discussion of the difficulties in determining satisfactory guidelines. The bibliography to this book lists numerous studies that discuss the problem of determining what constitutes an excessive market share. See especially Joe S. Bain, *Industrial Organization*, 2d ed. (New York: John Wiley & Sons, 1968), for a widely cited discussion of market shares; and C. Kaysen and D. F. Turner, *Antitrust Policy* (Cambridge: Harvard University Press, 1959), for one of the earliest proposals to impose limits on market shares.

[6] See Alfred F. Dougherty, Jr., "Statement before the Subcommittee on Energy and the Environment, Committee on the Interior, House of Representatives, on Horizontal Integration of Oil Companies," July 17, 1979.

The fundamental problem is that the concept of guidelines assumes the existence of a clear compartmentalization of the economy, which, as modern economic theory stresses, does not exist. Current economic theory stresses the interrelationship of markets and the impossibility of trying to separate the economy into isolated units. Concentration ratios, in contrast, assume the existence of such strong separation.

The theory of oligopoly stresses the inherent tension between the desire of firms to cooperate (explicitly or tacitly) to restrict competition and the formidable barriers to success in that effort. (To make market rigging difficult, U.S. law prohibits explicit collusion.) The theorists have been most successful in demonstrating that a large number of forces affect actual outcomes in imperfectly competitive markets. The possibilities have been shown to be too complex to permit predictions of whether a given situation is unsatisfactory. Therefore, it has not proved feasible to develop satisfactory indexes of the net effect of these forces. Some economists suspect there is a critical lack of tools for quantifying the entrepreneurial attitudes that play a large part in determining whatever competition or monopoly prevails in an industry.

Even when products are distinct, many questions arise about the geographic extent of markets. National data may either overstate the degree of monopoly by ignoring international competition or understate it by ignoring the isolation of some local businesses from external competition.

In short, the vigor of competition is generally difficult to determine and cannot in any case be deduced from analyzing something as simple as concentration ratios. Congress has therefore refrained from setting allowable concentration ratios in existing industries.

Economists and attorneys remain divided about the net social contribution of antitrust policies outside the price-fixing area, although there seems to be general agreement that price-fixing should be prohibited because it produces a monopolistic restriction of output without leading to more efficient production. But it is far less clear that policies to prevent mergers or to dismantle existing companies are socially beneficial. The legal action necessary to accomplish either of these goals is quite expensive for both parties. At best, the benefits may be small, and in cases where superior firms are sued to protect weaker ones, the outcome is likely to be harmful to society as a whole.

Although these views suggest a lack of enthusiasm for the DOJ guidelines and preference for eliminating the limits on total leasing and holding periods, there remains the question of what is optimal, given existing policy. The next chapter discusses that problem.

5

An Assessment of the Leasing Guidelines and Their Rationale

To develop its guidelines, the Department of Justice (DOJ) had to deal first with the issues of the extent to which different fuels compete and the geographic extent of markets. The department shared the concern raised by the Federal Trade Commission (FTC) about the fact that coal buyers generally seek a unified block of reserves to meet a long-term need for coal. Adequate competition, according to the Justice Department, should be defined in terms of whether control over reserves is sufficiently dispersed among numerous firms.

Overall, the guidelines are built upon a long chain of assumptions, many of which the department itself recognizes are open to question. We may begin with the most basic point first. At best, the department's guidelines establish the product-line, geographic, and reserve-availability dimensions of the market.

No one would dispute the need to determine whether a monopoly was developing in the relevant markets, whatever they may be. But the 10 and 15 percent ratios selected, as noted, have no basis in economic theory or empirical analysis. Thus, an arbitrarily selected ratio, even if applied to a correctly defined market, cannot determine if inadequate competition exists. The Justice Department, in effect, has sought a crutch on which to lean instead of simply deciding to monitor developments within the industry.

In its report the department itself notes the imperfection of concentration ratios as a measure. This point is almost lost, however, by the end of the report. The use of ratios becomes even more undesirable when questions about the adequacy of market definition are raised.

Before examining the key steps the DOJ's argument for the creation of guidelines, it may be useful to examine the state of the general debate over competition in energy. By now a vast literature has accumulated that discusses the extent of competition in U.S. energy industries, but there is no consensus on the issue. All the contentions that monopoly exists that I have encountered, however, appear in loosely structured discussions usually reflecting a distrust of business.[1] Any study that has taken a more analytic approach has concluded that coal and the other U.S. energy industries are highly competitive.[2] A better case for the existence of monopoly might be made, but the well-publicized efforts, such as those by Blair and Engler, have not provided it.

The inability of the analyses that disprove the existence of monopoly to attract attention, let alone convince people, suggests that formidable barriers exist to reducing public apprehensions about the possible existence of energy monopoly. These public apprehensions continue to exist despite the regularity with which agencies such as the DOJ, the FTC, and the General Accounting Office (GAO)—whose biases, if any, lie in seeking to maximize the problem of monopoly—conclude that it does not exist in the coal industry.[3]

The studies intended to prove the existence of monopoly rely primarily on hunches that the facts needed to prove their case are simply hidden by energy producers and their allies. In short, these studies contend that all of their suspicions about secret behavior within an industry must be refuted before the industry can be considered competitive. Given such a standard, any study that asserts the existence of vigorous competition can be dismissed as having failed to search thoroughly enough.

For present purposes, however, settling the debate conclusively is irrelevant. The critical consideration is that the DOJ's 1978 appraisal concluded that the coal industry was a vigorously competitive

---

[1] See U.S. Tennessee Valley Authority, *The Structure of the Energy Markets: A Report of TVA's Antitrust Investigation of the Coal and Uranium Industries* (Knoxville, 1977), and *The Structure of the Energy Markets: A Report of TVA's Antitrust Investigation of the Coal and Uranium Industries, 1979 Update* (Knoxville, 1979); John W. Wilson, "Report to the Director, Bureau of Competition, Federal Trade Commission, on 'Report to the Federal Trade Commission on the Structure of the Nation's Coal Industry' and 'Report to the Federal Trade Commission on Competition in the Nuclear Fuel Industry'" (Washington, D.C.: J. W. Wilson and Associates, 1978); John M. Blair, *The Control of Oil* (New York: Pantheon Books, 1976); and Robert Engler, *The Brotherhood of Oil* (Chicago: University of Chicago Press, 1977).

[2] See Thomas D. Duchesneau, *Competition in the U.S. Energy Industry* (Cambridge, Mass.: Ballinger, 1975), passim, footnote 7, and the references in footnote 30.

[3] U.S. Department of Justice, *Competition in the Coal Industry, 1978*, passim; Federal Trade Commission, *Structure of the Nation's Coal Industry*, passim; and U.S. General Accounting Office, *The State of Competition in the Coal Industry, 1977*.

industry. The 1978 study is the most comprehensively developed of the four appraisals of extensive statistical analyses of the coal industry undertaken by the FTC. The other three reviews include two by the FTC itself—one a draft report made available under the Freedom of Information Act and the other in the final FTC report—and one by the GAO.

Only the Justice Department report explicitly considers the question whether coal competes in a broader market that includes other fuels. The DOJ conclusion is that oil and natural gas are poor substitutes for coal but that some competition is offered by uranium. Doubts are expressed about the strength of this competition, however.

Two questions may be raised about the DOJ document. One concern of interest to the policy-making process is whether the department's estimate of oil and gas competition was valid. A more critical concern is the department's handling of competition between coal and nuclear power, since, in fact, the coal-leasing guidelines assume significant linkages between producers in the two fields.

The massive increase in oil and natural gas prices during the 1970s, which decreased the ability of these fuels to compete in the major markets for coal, and the failure of synthetic fuels industries based on coal to emerge have seriously weakened the argument that great substitutability exists among fuels.[4] Even the Tennessee Valley Authority's criticism of oil company participation in the coal industry contains the admission that oil does not compete with coal. The TVA's objections seem to rest on the suspicion that the oil companies will introduce superior skills at price fixing into the coal and nuclear industries.[5]

Although the DOJ report draws conclusions about competition between coal and nuclear power, supporting evidence for those conclusions is virtually absent. The only evidence provided is information on the collective market share in the coal industry of all the firms involved in various aspects of nuclear power and some qualitative statements about the degree of competition in various stages of the process that transforms uranium ore into reactor fuel. This does not tell us whether a few firms control both the coal and the uranium markets. Moreover, the report concludes that the position of nuclear-industry companies in the coal industry is too small to influence coal competition significantly and that no evidence exists that coal supplies have been withheld by nuclear or oil companies.

---

[4] See Thomas D. Duchesneau, *Interfuel Substitutability in the Electric Utility Sector of the U.S. Economy* (staff report to the Federal Trade Commission), 1972.
[5] See TVA, *Structure of the Energy Markets*, both reports.

What should also be noted is that an FTC report on the uranium industry concluded that concentration in that industry was not a serious problem and that there were few barriers to entry.[6] My own examinations of the uranium market in 1979 and 1980 suggest that prior studies understate, if anything, the potential for competition in uranium production. Numerous companies at home and abroad are ready to enter the uranium mining industry if the demand for new nuclear power plants improves.

The DOJ appears to accept this view and indicates that the problem lies in the stages of the process of converting uranium ore into reactor fuel. The two "bottleneck" states it cites are conversion and fuel-rod fabrication. Uranium is milled into a metal, but for the types of reactors used in the United States, the metal's content of U_{235} must be increased by enrichment. Before enrichment, therefore, the metal is converted into uranium fluoride. Only two firms, Kerr McGee and Allied Chemical, are engaged in conversion. After enrichment (a sector monopolized by the federal government), the enriched uranium must be enclosed in fuel rods for use in reactors. This kind of work is done by Exxon, by Gulf, and by four reactor manufacturers —General Electric, Westinghouse, Babcock and Wilcox, and Combustion Engineering.

It is inferred that these firms may have some degree of monopoly of power and thus their position in coal should be limited. Of these eight companies, however, only Kerr McGee, Exxon, Gulf, and General Electric are, in fact, engaged in coal production, and no data are provided to demonstrate that they have excessive shares of the market. Moreover, the Justice Department report fails to indicate whether the limited competition in the "bottleneck" areas is a problem or merely reflects the small size of the nuclear fuel industry.

The next issue is how to define the geographic scope of markets. The uranium market is worldwide, since transportation costs are so insignificant a part of uranium prices that mines with sufficiently low costs can compete anywhere in the world. The geographic scope of coal markets is local, however, and thus we are talking about competition between the world uranium market and local coal markets. To the extent that there is little coal-uranium competition, we may simply look at coal market structure, which is what the Justice Department did: it never considered the combined market, but it did examine the structure of the coal industry.

---

[6] See Joseph P. Mulholland, John Haring, and Stephen Martin, *An Analysis of Competitive Structure in the Uranium Supply Industry* (staff report to the Federal Trade Commission), 1979.

The DOJ's choice of market definitions seems to have been greatly affected by the FTC report, but the conclusions of the FTC and the GAO on the subject provide a contrast to the DOJ's policy posture. The FTC argued that originally there had been three main markets, those for Appalachian coal, Illinois basin coal, and western coal (largely in the Great Plains). But the FTC found that the penetration of western coal into the market for Illinois basin coal had created a combined Great Plains–Illinois basin market. The GAO accepted this view with the qualification that the southwestern portion of the western industry might be considered an isolated subsector.

The DOJ's position is that it is preferable to consider the Great Plains and the Illinois basin separate markets and to evaluate the Southwest separately. (That evaluation concludes, as did the GAO, that no problem exists in the southwestern coal market.)

The critical question is why the DOJ did not agree with the FTC and the GAO about the fusing of the Great Plains and Illinois basin into a single market. Some parts of the report suggest that the DOJ's position was based on a desire to show that even with a narrow definition of the market no evidence of anticompetitive conditions could be observed. Other comments suggest genuine doubts about a combined Great Plains–Illinois basin market, and the policy proposals are based on the implicit conclusion that the two regions do not strongly compete with each other. Thus, it is essential to decide whether the DOJ correctly determined the geographic scope of the coal markets.

The evidence for a combined Great Plains–Illinois basin market is that competition in the Midwest between Great Plains and Illinois basin coal producers is evident. The producers in the plains have so effectively captured the market in Minnesota—a market once predominantly served by Illinois basin coal—that Minnesota was treated by the DOJ as part of the market for the plains states. Furthermore, Montana and Wyoming coal was being used extensively in Illinois and Indiana. In 1978, 10.9 million of 33.0 million tons of coal delivered to electric utilities in Illinois came from Wyoming and Montana. In Indiana, 3.7 million of 30.5 million tons came from those two western states.[7]

The DOJ contention that the relevant market is the Great Plains in isolation seems to center on its interpretation of the debate inspired by Elzinger and Hogarty's proposed tests of whether regions are

---

[7] U.S. Department of Energy, Energy Information Administration, *Cost and Quality of Fuels for Electric Utility Plants—1978*, 1979, pp. 37–38.

linked.[8] Elzinger and Hogarty suggest that one should look at both imports and exports (with both terms defined, as in regional economics, to denote flows between areas rather than the narrower concept of flows only among countries). Interactions can occur either through importation of a commodity to a region or through exports to another region.

The DOJ expresses fears, however, that the inclusion of exports will overstate competition and that emphasis should be placed on imports. Parker and others oppose that argument on grounds that the exclusion of exports clearly omits important information about the scope of the market.[9] To state their case somewhat differently, the stronger of two regions of supply can be expected to have many exports and no imports. Customers will buy the coal with the cheapest delivered cost, and the market will be divided between the two suppliers at the point at which delivered prices are equal. By the nature of transportation economics, at every point nearer to, say, the Great Plains supplier than to the point of equal delivered prices, transportation costs will be lower, and customers will buy from the Great Plains supplier. Thus, if the point at which price equalization occurs is in the Midwest, everyone farther west will buy coal from the Great Plains, and it will have no imports.

The DOJ's concern seems to be that it is still possible that the local market could be monopolized by a supplier who would then engage in price discrimination, that is, a higher price for local sales than for export sales. This concern does not have much factual basis.[10] The local market is by far the least important market in long-term potential, and actual conditions are not favorable to discrimination. The degree of competition in the West is so great that coal suppliers fear their profits will prove inadequate. Moreover, customers are alert to market conditions and act vigorously to prevent price gouging by suppliers. Actions of buyers are reenforced by those of regulatory commissions, seeking to control energy costs. Moreover, many coal customers are, in fact, their own coal suppliers.

The interaction between the Great Plains and the Southwest is less clear. Although the potential for competition is considerable, movements of coal from the plains to the Southwest have not oc-

---

[8] See Kenneth G. Elzinger and Thomas M. Hogarty, "The Problem of Geographic Market Delineation Revisited: The Case of Coal," *Antitrust Bulletin*, vol. 23, no. 1 (Spring 1978), pp. 1–18.

[9] See Scott L. Parker et al., *An Analysis of Aspects of the Department of Justice's May 1978 Report on "Competition in the Coal Industry"* (Washington, D.C.: Management Analysis Center, 1979), pp. 3, 12–23, esp. pp. 14–17.

[10] Ibid., pp. 21, 42–50.

curred. All that has happened so far has been some shipments of both Great Plains and southwestern coal to Texas, but not necessarily to the same parts of the state.[11]

The whole idea of market segmentation may be quite inappropriate in the case of coal. The concept assumes that the only possible interactions are strong ones and that weaker interactions should be ignored. In fact, imperfect but important interactions occur to a degree that justifies believing that each part of the U.S. coal industry interacts indirectly with the other parts. The Illinois basin interacts with Appalachia as well as the plains. Just how much competition exists between the Illinois basin and Appalachia is open to question, but all three of the country's leading coal-using utilities—TVA, American Electric Power, and the Southern Company—are positioned so that they can and do buy coal from both Appalachia and the Illinois basin.

The next step in the two FTC reports, the GAO study, and the DOJ report was to provide information on the characteristics of the coal markets. In each case the appraisal was built primarily upon data assembled by the FTC on both the structure of the coal industry and the characteristics, such as the ability to acquire capital, that affect the ability to compete. Emphasis was placed on appraising the data on market shares, and each evaluation begins with a presentation of the conventional figures dealing with shares of production.

The FTC argued, however—and the DOJ and the GAO agreed—that the nature of the coal market was such that the conventional measures were not the most relevant. The FTC argued that coal mine development had become oriented toward supplying the needs of a specific customer over extended periods of time, such as the thirty-year useful life generally assumed for an electric power plant. Therefore, competition was best measured in terms of the number of suppliers available to serve new demands.

This led the FTC to develop the concept of shares of what may be called uncommitted available reserves. Reserve holdings of individual firms were related to total reserves that were not committed to any customers but had been made available to coal producers. The FTC considered unleased federal coal to be unavailable reserves.

My stated view that market share data of any sort are imperfect indicators of the vigor of competition implies that no good basis exists for appraising the data discussions in the reports. The important point to note is that the original FTC report, the GAO report, and the DOJ report all conclude that the evidence suggested that the coal industry was highly competitive and was likely to remain so, at least if the

---

[11] See Energy Information Administration, *Cost and Quantity of Fuels*, pp. 36–41.

leasing moratorium were ended. The final FTC report slightly muted the agency's views about the vigor of competition but on balance saw no great threats.

All the reports tend to overemphasize the market share data. In the DOJ report, the overemphasis was carried a step further by basing policy on the data on uncommitted reserve shares. The DOJ analysis should have been limited to the argument that the market share data and all other information implied that a highly competitive coal industry existed.

Applying the guidelines to uncommitted reserves is a particularly difficult task. Substantial uncertainties exist about the size of both the numerator and the denominator of market share fractions.

The DOJ points out that the U.S. Bureau of Mines estimate of demonstrated reserves has two major defects. The bureau's criteria for inclusion are criticized as exaggerating the amount of coal available at costs low enough to make the coal competitive, either today or at some time within the next several decades. Furthermore, the reserve base may be greatly understated because of incomplete geological assessment. The exclusion of at least the federal coal expected to be made available during the time over which the reserve holdings would be committed may have been appropriate for preparing estimates of the worst possible levels of concentration, but it seems inappropriate to ignore the role of such leasing in setting policy designed to guide leasing. Others would argue that all federal coal should be included, since it all could be leased if the desire to increase competition was strong enough.[12] But the DOJ argues that so long as it must set policy in a world of limited leasing in which a commitment to release federal coal to promote competition does not exist, coal unlikely to be leased must be ignored. Moreover, the Justice Department and the FTC, upon whom the DOJ depended for data, were concerned that their analysis might begin with an inadequate denominator.

The numerator also has defects, however. If the companies used the Bureau of Mines criteria, questions would arise about the economic position of company reserves. But Department of Energy discussions, confirmed by my discussions with industry sources, indicate that coal owners do not calculate reserves using those criteria.[13] Thus, it is clear that the FTC ratios are error-prone, but we cannot be sure whether the ratios are too high or too low.

---

[12] See Parker et al., *An Analysis*, pp. 34–35.

[13] See U.S. Department of Energy, Energy Information Administration, *EIA Symposium on Coal Resources/Reserves Information*, 1980, esp. pp. 128–45.

The most favorable situation for accepting the FTC ratios at face value occurs when the economic quality of the reserves held by each firm has the same distribution as the demonstrated reserve base, the firm reports demonstrated reserves using Bureau of Mines criteria, and the demonstrated reserve base is measured correctly. The problem of overstating the reserve base thus becomes irrelevant, since an exactly offsetting overstatement occurs with each firm's holdings.

Departures from these baseline assumptions can bias the results in either direction. To the extent that reserves as reported by the companies are better in quality than those in the reserve base, the shares are understated. Conversely, if company reserves are worse in quality and perhaps defined by a more generous inclusion standard than that of the Bureau of Mines, the shares are overstated. Understatement of total reserves leads to overstatement of shares. I would conjecture that the most probable situation is an overstatement of shares because of overestimates of company reserves and underestimates of total western coal resources.

Commitments to sell coal differ markedly. A mine supplying an existing facility is highly committed. At the other extreme, however, a tentative reservation of coal for synthetic fuel production may change at any time to a sale of the coal to more immediate customers.

Any attempt to determine the degree of the various types of commitments is complicated by a lack of data. The FTC survey used only information on the commitments of reserves by surveyed companies, leaving unknown the status of a substantial amount of coal. The FTC indicated that the reasonable range of assumptions was from stating that none of the unsurveyed coal was committed to stating that the proportional commitment of unsurveyed coal was equal to that of surveyed coal. The premise for the upper limit is that, by the very nature of the survey process, those companies that were included were those most likely to have made commitments. Thus, the excluded companies could not have commitment ratios higher than the included ones. The DOJ adopted the assumption of equal commitment of both reported and unreported reserves by owners to ensure conservatism in its analysis.

Thus, the key defects of the DOJ guidelines are that they use debatable and probably unduly restrictive definitions of the relevant market and rely on defective measures of the shares of uncommitted coal held.

The railroad restrictions are similarly illogical. Here, the guiding viewpoint is that transportation supply is restricted to produce monopoly prices but that rail rates cannot be raised to the monopoly price because of rate regulation. The railroads can, however, mine and sell coal at a price that includes the monopoly profits that would be produced by restricting transportation supply. What the Justice Department fails to consider is how the railroads could monopolize the coal supply to reap these profits.

At this point, it is necessary to return to the question of guidelines for companies in the bottleneck stages of nuclear power. It has already been argued that the DOJ did not provide any factual basis for its concern. The present discussion examines the theoretical arguments presented by the DOJ.

The department presents two special theories of monopoly—"kickback" and "withholding." In both cases the basic concept is that a market exists that involves competition among the producers of two or more different commodities. Economic theory would predict that price rigging would occur only if a firm or closely knit group of firms held a large share of the combined market for these commodities. The only possibility of large shares is through substantial participation in the production of one commodity (and little production of the other) or through significant production of several of the linked commodities.

On close examination, the concept of the kickback turns out to be nothing but a special name for market power consisting principally of participation in the production of one commodity. Withholding is a similarly unneeded term for power through participation in the production of several commodities.

A particularly weak point in the DOJ theory of kickback monopoly is the version in which there is monopoly in one industry and competition in the other. Norman suggested that if this were the case, actions in the competitive industry would undermine any efforts at monopolizing the other industry.[14] The problem seems to be the proper interpretation of just what the DOJ meant by competition in the other industry. If we take the department literally and assume unlimited freedom of entry in one sector, Norman's conclusion will be the proper one. The Justice Department's argument can be "saved" only by asserting that competition means lack of market power by existing firms but limited freedom of entry. This is a curious definition of competition.

Indeed, John H. Shenefield, then assistant attorney general in charge of the DOJ antitrust division, has noted that "increased demand for coal would have little effect on coal prices" because the

---

[14] See Donald Norman, "Competition in the Coal Industry: Review and Critique" (Washington, D.C.: American Petroleum Institute, 1978).

suppliers are so numerous.[15] Shenefield stated this when opposing the application of the kickback (or withholding) theory to oil company participation in the coal industry. The contention also applies to the use of the kickback theory to rationalize special rules for nuclear companies. Shenefield's statement suggests that the DOJ's faith in the applicability of its kickback and withholding theories to coal is not sufficient to justify special limits for companies in the bottleneck stages of uranium processing.

What, then, is justified? I would argue for nothing more than careful governmental monitoring of competition in the coal industry and governmental intervention when positive evidence is obtained that firms are accumulating excessive shares of truly marketable reserves.

The DOJ may argue that legal precedents compel it to adopt stringent guidelines, but the evidence cited above suggests that available data are grossly inadequate for constructing a mechanistic approach to the regulation of leasing. I can see no reason why the DOJ should not be content with stringent enforcement on a case-by-case basis. The law, it may be recalled, calls for review of specific leases. The guidelines would simply make review easier for the DOJ. This limited benefit would come at the cost of adding still another impediment to the expeditious development of energy production. In short, the cost would undoubtedly exceed the benefits.

---

[15] See the processed version of his "Testimony Before the Subcommittee on Energy and the Environment of the Committee on Interior and Insular Affairs, United States House of Representatives, Concerning H.R. 8, the Public Energy Competition Act," 1979.

Bibliography

Anderson, Frederick R., et al. *Environmental Improvement through Economic Incentives.* Baltimore: Johns Hopkins University Press for Resources for the Future, 1977.

Bain, Joe S. *Industrial Organization.* 2d ed. New York: John Wiley & Sons, 1968.

Blair, John M. *The Control of Oil.* New York: Pantheon Books, 1976.

————. *Economic Concentration: Structure, Behavior, and Public Policy.* New York: Harcourt Brace Jovanovich, 1972.

Borts, George H. "Verified Statement." In *Statements of Facts and Argument of Union Electric Company, Wisconsin Electric Company, Wisconsin Power & Light Company, and Wisconsin Public Service Corporation before the Interstate Commerce Commission, Increased Rates on Coal, Midwestern Railroad, August 1979* (Docket 37246 and Sub. nos. 1–6 and Consolidated Cases 37348 and 37353), 1980.

Dougherty, Alfred F., Jr. "Statement before the Antitrust and Monopoly Subcommittee on the Judiciary, United States Senate, on Horizontal Integration of Oil Companies," 1978. Processed.

————. "Statement before the Subcommittee on Energy and the Environment, Committee on the Interior, House of Representatives, on Horizontal Integration of Oil Companies," July 17, 1979. Processed.

Duchesneau, Thomas D. *Competition in the U.S. Energy Industry.* Cambridge, Mass.: Ballinger, 1975.

————. *Interfuel Substitutability in the Electric Utility Sector of the U.S. Economy.* Staff report to the Federal Trade Commission, 1972.

Elzinger, Kenneth G., and Hogarty, Thomas F. "The Problem of Geographic Market Delineation Revisited: The Case of Coal." *Antitrust Bulletin* 23:1 (Spring 1978): 1–18.

Engler, Robert. *The Brotherhood of Oil: Energy Policy and the Public Interest.* Chicago: University of Chicago Press, 1977.

Exxon U.S.A. (W. T. Slick). Letter to John H. Shenefield (with

October 23 reply by Donald L. Flexner, U.S. Department of Justice), 1979.

Gordon, Richard L. *Coal in the U.S. Energy Market: History and Prospects.* Lexington, Mass.: Lexington Books, 1978.

―――. *Economic Analysis of Coal Supply: An Assessment of Existing Studies.* Final Report, vol. 3. Palo Alto: Electric Power Research Institute, 1979.

―――. "Hobbling Coal—Or How to Serve Two Masters Poorly." *Regulation* 2:1 (July/August 1978): 36–45.

―――. "The Hobbling of Coal: Policy and Regulatory Uncertainties." *Science* 200 (April 14, 1978): 153–58.

ICF, Inc. *Coal and Electric Utilities Model Documentation.* (Amended version of ICF, Inc., *The National Coal Model: Description and Documentation,* 1976.) Washington, D.C., 1977.

―――. *The Demand for Western Coal and Its Sensitivity to Key Uncertainties.* Washington, D.C., 1978.

―――. *Effects of Alternative New Source Performance Standards for Coal-Fired Electric Utility Boilers on the Coal Market and on Utility Capacity Expansion Plans.* Washington, D.C., 1978.

―――. *Effects of No Further Leasing on the Nation's Coal Markets.* Washington, D.C., 1979.

―――. *The Final Set of Analyses of Alternative New Source Performance Standards for New Coal-Fired Power Plants.* Washington, D.C., 1979.

―――. *Further Analysis of Alternative New Source Performance Standards for New Coal-Fired Power Plants.* Washington, D.C., 1978.

―――. *Observation on Fair Market Value for Federal Coal Leases.* Washington, D.C., 1979.

―――. *Still Further Analyses of Alternative New Source Performance Standards for New Coal-Fired Power Plants.* Washington, D.C., 1979.

Kaysen, C., and Turner, D. F. *Antitrust Policy.* Cambridge: Harvard University Press, 1959.

Kneese, Allen V., and Schultze, Charles L. *Pollution, Prices, and Public Policy.* Washington, D.C.: Brookings Institution, 1975.

Landsberg, Hans H., et al. *Energy: The Next Twenty Years.* Report by a study group sponsored by the Ford Foundation and administered by Resources for the Future. Cambridge, Mass.: Ballinger, 1979.

McDonald, Stephen L. *The Leasing of Federal Lands for Fossil Fuels Production.* Baltimore: Johns Hopkins University Press for Resources for the Future, 1979.

Markham, Jesse W. "The Competitive Effects of Joint Bidding by Oil Companies for Offshore Oil Leases." In *Industrial Organization and Economic Development,* edited by Jesse W. Markham and G. F. Papanek. Boston: Houghton Mifflin, 1970.

Mead, Walter J. "Federal Public Lands Leasing Policies." *Quarterly of the Colorado School of Mines* 64:4 (October 1969): 187–214.

Mead, Walter, et al. *Competition and Performance in OCS Oil and Gas Lease Sales and Lease Development, 1954–1969.* Reston, Va.: U.S. Geological Survey, 1980.

Mills, Edwin S. *The Economics of Environmental Quality.* New York: W. W. Norton, 1978.

Mulholland, Joseph P.; Haring, John; and Martin, Stephen. *An Analysis of Competitive Structure in the Uranium Supply Industry.* Washington, D.C.: U.S. Federal Trade Commission, 1979. (Also draft version on file in the Federal Trade Commission library.)

Musgrave, Richard A. *The Theory of Public Finance.* New York: McGraw-Hill, 1959.

National Research Council, Committee on Nuclear and Alternative Energy Systems. *Energy in Transition 1985–2010.* San Francisco: W. H. Freeman, 1980.

Navarro, Peter. "The Politics of Air Pollution." *The Public Interest* 59 (Spring 1980): 36–44.

Norman, Donald. "Competition in the Coal Industry: Review and Critique." Washington, D.C.: American Petroleum Institute, 1978.

Ogden, Daniel M., Jr. "Protecting Energy Turf: The Department of Energy Organization Act," *Natural Resources Journal* 18 (October 1978): 845–57.

Parker, Scott L., et al. *An Analysis of Aspects of the Department of Justice's May 1978 Report on "Competition in the Coal Industry."* Washington, D.C.: Management Analysis Center, 1979.

Portney, Paul R., ed. *Current Issues in U.S. Environmental Policy.* Baltimore: Johns Hopkins University Press for Resources for the Future, 1978.

Samuelson, Paul A. *The Collected Scientific Papers of Paul A. Samuelson.* 4 vols. Cambridge: MIT Press, 1966, 1972 and 1977.

Scherer, F. M. *Industrial Market Structure and Economic Performance.* 2d ed. Chicago: Rand McNally College Publishing Company, 1980.

Shenefield, John H. "Testimony before the Subcommittee on Energy and the Environment of the Committee on Interior and Insular Affairs, United States House of Representatives, Concerning H.R. 8, the Public Energy Competition Act," 1979. Processed.

Shepherd, William G. *The Economics of Industrial Organization.* Englewood Cliffs, N.J.: Prentice Hall, 1979.

Stobaugh, Robert, and Yergin, Daniel, eds. *Energy Future.* Report of the Energy Project at the Harvard Business School. New York: Random House, 1979.

U.S. Bureau of Land Management. *Final Environmental Statement, Federal Coal Management Program.* 1979.

U.S. Congress. *Public Law 94-377, An Act to Amend the Mineral Leasing Act of 1920, and for Other Purposes* (the Mineral Leasing Amendment Act of 1976), 1976.

U.S. Congress. House of Representatives. *Clean Air Amendments of 1977, Conference Report, Report No. 95-564,* 1977.

U.S. Department of Energy, Energy Information Administration. *Cost and Quantity of Fuels for Electric Utility Plants—1978,* 1979.

———. *EIA Symposium on Coal Resources/Reserves Information,* 1980. See esp. pp. 128–45.

U.S. Department of the Interior. *Federal Coal Management Report, Fiscal Year 1979,* 1980.

———. *Final Environmental Impact Statement, Proposed Federal Coal Leasing Program,* 1974.

———. *Secretarial Issue Document: Federal Coal Management Program,* 1979.

U.S. Department of Justice. *Competition in the Coal Industry,* 1978.

———. "Merger Guidelines of the Department of Justice," 1969.

U.S. Federal Trade Commission. *Report to the Federal Trade Commission on the Structure of the Nation's Coal Industry,* 1978. (Also draft version available in Federal Trade Commission library.)

U.S. General Accounting Office. *The State of Competition in the Coal Industry,* 1977.

U.S. Tennessee Valley Authority (Herbert S. Sanger and William E. Mason). *The Structure of the Energy Markets: A Report of TVA's Antitrust Investigation of the Coal and Uranium Industries,* 3 vols. Knoxville, 1977.

———. *The Structure of the Energy Markets: A Report of TVA's Antitrust Investigation of the Coal and Uranium Industries, 1979 update.* Knoxville, 1979.

Wilson, Carroll L. *Coal Bridge to the Future.* Report of the World Coal Study. Cambridge, Mass.: Ballinger, 1980.

Wilson, John W. "Report to the Director, Bureau of Competition, Federal Trade Commission, on 'Report to the Federal Trade Commission on the Structure of the Nation's Coal Industry' and 'Report to the Federal Trade Commission on Competition in the Nuclear Fuel Industry.'" Washington, D.C.: J. W. Wilson and Associates, 1978.